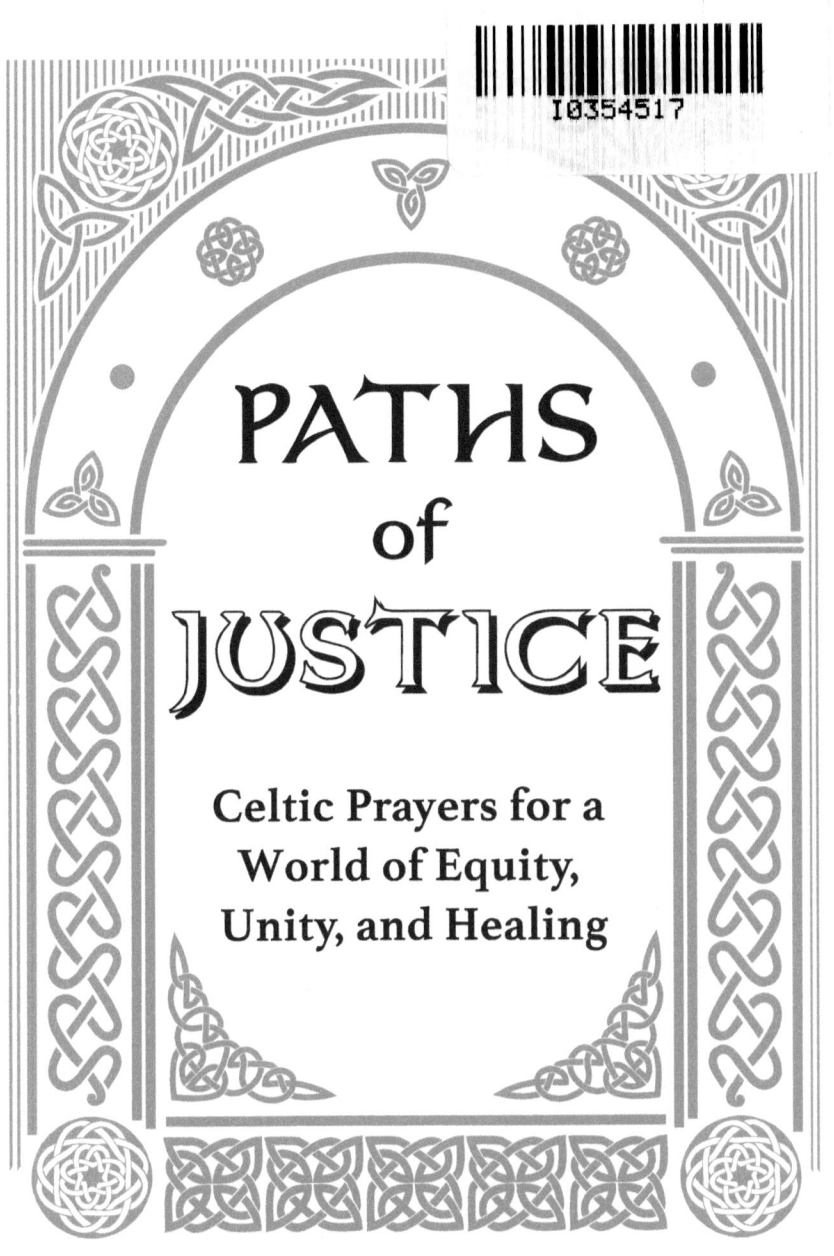

PATHS of JUSTICE

Celtic Prayers for a World of Equity, Unity, and Healing

PATHS of JUSTICE

Celtic Prayers for a
World of Equity,
Unity, and Healing

RAY SIMPSON

Anamchara Books

PATHS OF JUSTICE
Celtic Prayers for a World of Equity, Unity, and Healing

Copyright © 2023, Anamchara Books.

All rights reserved. No part of this publication may be reproduced or transmitted for commercial purposes, except for brief quotations, without written permission of the publisher. Churches and other noncommercial interests may reproduce portions of this book without the express written permission of Anamchara Books, provided that the text does not exceed 500 words or 5 percent of the entire book, whichever is less, and that the text is not material quoted from another publisher. When reproducing text from this book, include the following credit line: "From *Paths of Justice: Celtic Prayers for a World of Equity, Unity, and Healing*, published by Anamchara Books. Used by permission."

Anamchara Books
Vestal, New York 13850
www.AnamcharaBooks.com

IngramSpark paperback edition ISBN: 978-1-62524-870-1 eBook ISBN: 978-1-62524-863-3

Scripture quotations are the editor's own translations, using the literal meanings and implications of the original Bible languages.

God watches and protects
the paths of justice.

—Proverbs 2:8

CONTENTS

1. Prayers of Confession	9
2. Prayer for the Wise Use of Resources	23
3. Prayers for Building Bridges	35
4. Prayers to the Divine in One Another	53
5. Prayers for Welcome and Help	69
6. Prayers of Self-Surrender	83
7. Prayers for Energy and Empowerment	99
8. Prayers of Blessing	113
Endnotes	141

Prayers of Confession

The first step on the road to transformation is confession. The church teaches that—and so do many psychologists. We cannot begin to change, either individually or as a society, until we acknowledge where we have gone wrong. The root word of *confess* is the Latin *confessare*, which means "to utter, to speak aloud"—and for Carl Jung and other depth psychologists, as for most Christians, confession involves not only facing our wrongdoing but also expressing it in spoken words to another person.

The Oxford English Dictionary defines "to confess" as "to declare or disclose something which one has kept or allowed to remain secret as being prejudicial or inconvenient to oneself; to acknowledge, own or admit; to make one's self known, to disclose one's identity." This is seldom fun. We do not like to confront our mistakes and failures; we like even less revealing them to others. We often do not want to admit, even to ourselves, that our identities contain selfishness and greed—and those qualities in our own hearts have damaged others, including our larger society. It's easier, at least in the short run, to avoid these uncomfortable truths. "What's done is done," we may say. "No point crying over spilt milk."

But as it turns out, there *is* a point to crying over the spilt milk. When we face the consequences of our actions and express our sorrow and remorse, we open a space for change to occur. We cannot erase what we have done in the past, but we can seek ways in the future to restore and heal what has gone awry. The milk can't be unspilled—but we can work to find ways to clean up the mess. As Jungian analyst Margaret Krenk wrote: "Confession is the culmination of one inner drama and the initiation of another. Confession is the vector through which psychic energy moves from the past into the future.... Confession is how souls open to the healing power of grace."[1]

In this chapter, Ray Simpson gives us prayers of confession that can be our first steps onto paths of justice. He makes clear that confession is not about wallowing in guilt and shame. Instead, as we face where we have done wrong, individually and as a society, we open a door for the Spirit's transformative power to enter both our own lives and the larger world as well.

The person who tries to hide the times
she has broken trust with others will be held back,
unable to thrive or live a victorious life
of prosperity and wholeness.
But if she confesses her wrongdoing
and leaves it behind her,
God will help her to grow and become whole,
for Divine mercy offers the all-encompassing love
and nourishment of a mother's womb.

—Proverbs 28:13

Arbiter of the nations,
we confess that the twin evils
of power and greed
have often usurped Your values
and torn us apart.
Humble our proud pretensions
and forgive us our selfishness.
Replace our military walls
with sacred, hospitable space.
Move us to build cities of friendship
between races and religions.
Raise up a new generation of leaders
who are guided by love and justice.
Forgive us for the oppression and violence
we have condoned with our silence.
Give our nation a soul that honours You
by honouring one another.

Almighty God,
nothing on earth can compare to You,
nothing on earth can contain You.
You always keep Your promises,
and so we ask for Your forgiveness
for we have harmed our neighbours
and oppressed the innocent,
but You have promised
that if we turn again to You,
You will forgive us and restore us.
Send us rain and revive the crops
we have damaged with our own
selfishness and ignorance.
We come to You,
we who have warred and wasted the land,
confessing and asking for forgiveness.
Forgive us for failing to welcome foreigners,
for doing violence to one another,
and for imprisoning the innocent.

Hear from heaven, we pray;
forgive us,
and heal both our hearts
and our land.

(Inspired by King Solomon's prayer in 2 Chronicles 6.)

All-Powerful and All-Compassionate One,
we confess we have worshipped the false gods
of fortune, fame, and fantasy.
Remind us we have to reap what we sow.
May we turn from our selfish ways
and serve You as the living God
who works without ceasing
for love and justice.

We bless You, Life-Giver,
for Your covenant of renewal with Noah.
We confess we have failed to do our part.
Renew our relationship with the Earth.
We bless You for Your covenant of justice with Moses.
We confess we have failed to keep up our end.
Establish Your justice in the world.
We bless You for Your covenant of intimacy with David.
We confess we have failed to extend
that intimacy to others.
Extend Your Spirit through our communities.
We bless You for Your covenant of love with Jesus.
We confess we have failed to love one another.
Heal our relationships with one another..

We confess, Creator, that we have used
more of the Earth's resources than was our share.
As we face the consequences of greed and ignorance,
may we learn to live more simply
that others may simply live,
to produce sustainably, to invest ethically,
and to live as responsible members
of a community that has no borders,
that includes each form of life
upon the Earth.

We confess that we have acted unjustly;
we pray for an end to the injustices
that become the breeding grounds of war.
We confess that we have turned away
from our sisters and brothers
and built walls between our hearts and theirs;
we pray for the restoration of fellowship
and the building of integrity.
We confess that we have been selfish;
we pray for commitment
to the unending struggle against selfish ways
and the violations of human dignity.
We confess that we have created
a world of violence and inequity;
we pray for that peace
which is the full and healthy blossoming
of what human life was meant to be.

We confess our conflicts,
our brutality, and our cruelty.
You whose order rules the atom,
You whose law propels the sea,
bring the nations, drowned in discord
closer to Your harmony.
God of beauty, heal our sickness;
God of love, our fractures mend.
Foster unity that binds us,
rich to poor and foe to friend.

Prayer for the Wise Use of Resources

All indigenous cultures around the world, including the Celts, have honored Nature. Ancient Celts worked the land but they did not regard it as a possession; taking care of the land's resources—including its trees, plants, creatures, soil, and stones—was a way for the community to take care of each other. In India, tradition dictates that for every tree cut, people need to plant five trees. In Australia, indigenous people protect the health of mangrove areas by only hunting there for a few months every year and then giving the groves time to recover. The Tonga people of Zambia practice crop rotation and other techniques for protecting the soil's fertility. In North America, the Chippewa and many other tribal nations are building housing, colleges, and veteran homes that use geothermal and wind energy. As indigenous ethnobotanist Linda Black Elk said, "Standing in right relationship changes the way we walk on the landscape. When we know the trees, herbs, birds, and other living things as our relatives, we treat them with kindness and respect, we practice reciprocity and sustainability. Practicing sustainability is the best way to protect both people and our Mother Earth."²

This attitude of treating Nature as sacred, a Divine gift, needs to be revived in the Western world. We Westerners, however, have had a utilitarian approach to Nature. We see it as existing separate from human beings, and we treat trees and soil, ore and oil, creatures and crops as commodities that exist purely for our convenience. We need to open our hearts and minds to the ancient indigenous ways, which recognized the Earth as our mother and treated her with respect, honoring the reciprocal relationships contained within her web of life.

"Sustainability requires the planting of seeds today," wrote Jenna Grey-Eagle, "the benefits of which we might not experience in our own lifetime."³ As Westerners, however, we have allowed our selfishness to rule our environmental practices. As a result, we have used far more than our share of the planet's resources, and now all of us—but especially people of color living in poverty—are bearing the consequences of our ravaged word. "Climate change will affect the basic elements of life for people around the world, food production, health, and the environment," reported Nicholas Stern. "Hundreds of millions of people could suffer hunger, water shortages and coastal flooding as the world warms."[4] Plants, animals, and other human beings bear the mortal cost of our lifestyle. As theologian Matthew Fox reminds us, "Sustainability is another word for justice, for what is just is sustainable and what is unjust is not."[5]

May the prayers in this chapter remind us to change our attitudes and actions—and may the Creator empower us with the wisdom and energy we need to care for and conserve our planet's rich resources.

*We must say of the universe
that it is a communion of subjects,
not a collection of objects.*

—THOMAS BERRY[6]

Father, You give us many gifts
that we may share them
in the work of building up Your people.
Help us to receive deeply,
and to give ourselves generously,
that in the work to which You call us
we may know the wonder of Your presence
in another human life.

God of the Divine Economy—
the whole created universe—
teach us to use money
as a servant of the common good.
Teach us to use the market
as a guide, not as a god.
Teach us to invest
in what brings long-term well-being
to the planet and its people.
And teach us to recognize the cheats
dressed in sheep's clothing
and expose them for what they are.

Beloved One,
we long to dwell always in Your presence,
so help us to:
speak the truth from our hearts;
keep gossip from our tongues;
do nothing but good to our friends;
keep our promises
(even when they cost us time or money);
bless others in our use of money;
and refuse to let our resources be used
in any way that hurts others;
that we grow ever more secure in You,
as we put our trust in You,
rather than in our resources.

(Inspired by Psalm 15.)

Vast and Giving One,
wean us from our attachment to possessions.
Forgive our nation for bingeing on loans
our children must repay.
Cure our addiction to debt.
Grant us mercy as we reap what we have sown.
May we not forget
the abundance You have shared with us,
and make us willing
to share Your gifts with others.

God bless the Earth's oil
and the good things it has made possible.
God forgive us for grabbing it
and wasting it without wisdom.
God help us
as we reap the harvest of our misdeeds.
God guide us
as we seek to harness the energies
of sun and wind and water,
and make us wise enough
to heal the planet of the harm we have dealt it.
God make us generous
with the Earth's resources,
recognizing they are not ours to own or hoard.

Good God,
may we never take for granted
the blessings of prosperity and peace,
and may we work to share those blessings
with those who have less.
May we not grow lazy
in the struggle against greed,
neglect, and injustice.
May our nation be freed
from the bondage of fear,
and may she rise above selfish ambition,
and become flexible to Your direction.
May the qualities
that make democracy function
flourish:
faithfulness to one another,
honesty,
and the willingness to share.

Our society is ever restless,
always craving one more thing to do,
seeking happiness through more and more:
more possessions,
more money,
more prestige.
Teach us to be at peace with what we have,
to embrace what we have received,
and to know that enough is enough.
May our restless greed and striving cease
so we rest content in You alone.

Prayers for Building Bridges

Polarization has ruptured our world. Conservatives dislike liberals, and liberals dislike conservatives. Christians distrust Muslims, and Muslims distrust Christians. Whites fear Blacks, and Blacks (with good reason) fear whites. What started out as small cracks in our society have expanded into deep chasms. Terror-stricken and angry, we stare at each across the gaping fissures—and instead of building bridges, we erect walls of self-protection that make it even harder for us to reach out and take one another's hands.

But when Jesus said, "Blessed are the peacemakers" (Matthew 5:9), I believe he was calling us to be bridge-builders. Bridge-building requires that we ask forgiveness, that we seek and see commonality even as we open ourselves to new ideas and experiences different from our own. Bridge-building calls for humility and the willingness to change. It asks us to set aside our fears and anger, as we follow in the footsteps of Jesus (who came to earth as the eternal bridge between the Creator and humanity).

Our world is full of crises—global climate change, racism, pandemics, and wars, to name just a few—and we will never solve them unless we begin to work together instead of against each other. May Ray Simpson's prayers in this chapter inspire us and teach us to span the divisions between us. May the Life-Giver unite us in love and hope.

A person who thinks only about building walls,
wherever they may be,
and not building bridges, is not Christian.
This is not in the Gospel.

—Pope Francis

Help us bring to birth a civilization
inspired by love
and the values of respect and freedom,
the values of Aidan and Hilda.
Help us clear out the power and greed
that have usurped these values
and torn us apart.
Raise up a new generation
of Divinely inspired leaders.
Restore fellowship
between peoples of all skin colors and all faiths.
Replace our barriers with hospitable space.
Inspired by trailblazers
and bridge-builders of the past,
make us trailblazers and bridge-builders today.

Divine Father,
help us to affirm the good in others.
Divine Friend,
help us to reach out warmly to others.
Divine Spirit,
help us to connect well with others
across the shores that separate.

Life-Giver, we would like to be
part of a nursery of saints.
Show us what needs to happen for this to be,
so that we can nurture others to know You better.
May our lives be a seedbed of prayer and of friendship
lived out in fellowship with others,
building bridges across
whatever separates us.

We pray, Beloved, for children and young people.
Help us to encourage them,
to listen to their thoughts and see their pictures.
Help us to humbly receive what they tell us,
and to keep at least half an ear cocked
for Your voice coming to us through them.
We pray for the youth of our own and other lands
who lack purpose and identity,
creating a vacuum that tyranny could fill.
Raise up enablers and motivators.
May Christ-followers and seekers of justice
find connecting points with young people
upon which to build mentoring and solidarity.
We pray for conflict resolvers and trust builders.
Help us to turn things around.

All-forgiving One,
when I meet angry people
who carry centuries of oppression,
neglect, or mistreatment,
help me to listen to their stories
without judgement or interruption,
without erecting my defenses,
and may they know
that they have met someone
who has deeply listened,
who was willing to build a bridge
across the past injuries that separate us.

Dear Life-Giver,
what pleasure it gives You
when we reflect in our relationships
the love You and Jesus and the Spirit
have for one another and for us.
We know that we are only as near to You
as we are to the people
from whom we are most divided.
We pray for those people we are furthest from.
In our hearts, we reach out to them,
and in our lives, we work to build new bridges
of friendship and understanding.
You are pleased
when divisions are healed,
and we are pleased
when unity with one another is restored.

Bind us together,
Giver of Life,
bind us together,
bind us together in love.
We are one family of God,
sisters and brothers in Christ,
called to give love to the world.
Draw us nearer our Head,
so that Your Spirit is the bridge
that connects us all
to one another.

Crucified Jesus,
You lived and died a Jew
with love in Your heart toward all.
Risen Christ,
You appeared under open skies
to those who did not recognize You.
Teach us to see past our differences,
to build bridges of understanding
that span the boundaries
our doctrines and dogma have erected.
May we follow Your example,
and make love the envoy
that's willing to always see
from another's point of view.

May we make common cause
with those who do right.
May we not make a fuss
about where good comes from.
May we stop creating divisions
built on doctrine and belief
and let God look after God,
while we do God's work on earth.

God of Unity,
help us to build bridges of peace:
peace between believers and nonbelievers;
peace between neighbours and strangers;
peace between lovers and enemies.
Creator of all life,
help us to build bridges of love:
love between person and person;
love between wife and husband;
love between parents and children;
the love of Christ that draws us all together.
Create, we pray,
understanding between political parties,
understanding between factions and perspectives,
understanding between religious traditions,
between generations,
between rich and poor,
between all skin colors and ethnic backgrounds,
and between victor and vanquished.

The peace of Christ above all peace,
the love of Christ greater than all love,
and the understanding of Christ
beyond all understanding
build new bridges of possibility
in our communities
and in our world.

Remind us, God of Love,
that when we eagerly desire
the best for one another,
the differences between us
no longer seem as important.
Knowing that we share the same origin,
the same essence,
and the same journey together
away from fragmentation,
may we work with You
toward the completion of all things
and all people,
so that in Christ,
we might be reunited
in love.

God of the rainbow,
may our many colours,
temperaments, shapes, and sizes
come together
through the rain and sunshine
pouring from Your Spirit,
so that we are united and transformed
into a rainbow coalition
whose glory is beyond our imagining.

Prayers to the Divine in One Another

"Each person is not just to be respected but to be revered as one created in God's image," wrote Desmond Tutu. "To treat a child of God as if he or she was less than this is not just wrong, which it is; it is not just evil, as it often is; not just painful, as it often must be for the victim; it is veritably blasphemous, for it is to spit in the face of God."[7] Every person, no matter how dissimilar to us or unlikeable they may seem, carries the image of God. To ignore any part of the human family, either as a group or as individuals, is to ignore an aspect of God.

The Great Heart of the Universe calls us into a new relationship with people who share our lives and our world. As we see them with new eyes, we perceive the image of God. The goodness and beauty we find in each other draws us ever deeper into the goodness and beauty of God. We realize we are each beloved and precious.

As we enter into relationships based on justice and equality, we stand in awe before the Divine Presence in each other. We see and affirm others' beauty, strength, and gifts. We allow God's love to flow from us out into the world, and at the same time, we open our hearts to receive Divine love as it comes to us through other humans. We enter into a spirit of giving that excludes no one, and as we mutually give and receive, we create a world of integrity, kindness, and fair play.

May the prayers Ray Simpson wrote for this chapter open our eyes to the Divine presence in each individual we encounter.

Every human life is a reflection of divinity,
and . . . every act of injustice mars
and defaces the image of God in [humanity].

—MARTIN LUTHER KING JR.[8]

There is no dichotomy between [humans] and God's image.
Whoever tortures a human being,
whoever abuses a human being,
whoever outrages a human being,
abuses God's image.

—OSCAR ROMERO[9]

Word of God, rays from You
light people of many beliefs.
May these rays lead us
to the places where we may sit
and eat and be one
with those who are different from us,
until You emerge in their clothes,
revealing a new facet
of Your never-ending glory.

May Your tender love burn inside us
and impel us on the road to seek for Christ
in the stranger's face
or, sensing his absence,
introduce his presence.

Jesus, You were born into a world of oppression;
You are with us in oppression.
Jesus, You were born into a world
where the innocent were killed;
You are with us when innocent ones are killed.
Jesus, You were a refugee in Egypt;
You are with everyone who has to flee their homeland.
Jesus, You were broken on the Cross;
be with us Your broken people.

Make us pilgrims of the world
until we see Your face in everyone we meet.
Make us pilgrims of the grail
until we see Your grace in every place we visit,
Make us pilgrims of the road
until we see Your prints in every chore we do.

Birther and Arbiter of the human family,
who delights in our diversity,
teach us to see a new facet of Your Being
in each person we meet.
Teach us to live by Your law of love,
to find the dignity of diversity,
and see Your Presence
in those who are different from ourselves.

God of shepherds and angels,
as Hilda drew out the songs
that were locked in shy Caedmon's heart,
may we draw out the music
that lies buried in a thousand lives:
the music of speech and seeing;
the music of laughter and loving;
the music of craft and creating.
May we open new doors
for Your Spirit to enter our world
by empowering others to use their gifts,
until all Creation comes alive
with the Song of Your love.

God who dances with Creation,
planting Your likeness in each one of us,
send us out to fill the world with love,
rejoicing in Your reflection
in every soul we meet.

Yahweh,

people call You by a hundred names,

but You simply

ARE.

Help us to simply

BE,

and in our

BEING,

out of the silence of a listening heart,

may compassion and rapport with others grow.

Teach us to sense Your

BEING

in one another.

Out of the sharing of our treasures,

may others see You

ARE,

and may You have all the glory.

High King, Creator of all,
remind us that every human life is sacred,
whether it belongs to a woman in a war-torn land,
a disabled person next door,
a child on our borders,
or a terminally ill patient.
Remind us that whatever a person's age,
appearance, or beliefs,
each individual carries Your likeness,
and Christ is revealed in each one.
Every person is precious in Your sight.

Ground of All Being,
all people come from You,
and all people have some of You in them.
As we see Your image in one another,
may we honour and seek
the common good of each person.
Unity of the World,
from You all peace, all justice flow.
May we cherish the web of life
that reveals Your Spirit.

Christ Jesus,
by sharing our lives on earth,
You declared every life to be sacred.
You confirmed the Creator's image in each person.
Imbue us with deep respect for every individual.
May we recognize and value
the many roles and gifts
that are needed to sustain
a cohesive world.

Prayers for Welcome and Help

"Treat the stranger who lives in your midst the same way you treat everyone else," God says to Moses in the Book of Leviticus. "Love her in the same way you love yourself, for you too have been a stranger." We have all been "strangers" at one time or another (in gym class in middle school, when you were the class klutz among the jocks, for example—or when you were the new employee on your first day at work or you moved to a new neighborhood where you felt as though you shared nothing in common with anyone). Remember that feeling—and then remember what a relief it was when someone smiled at you, asked you to share their lunch table, or reached out a hand in friendship.

Too often, though, we see strangers as . . . well, *strange*. We notice their differences, and we fear they will be a threat to us in some way. We feel justified in saying we don't want "their sort" in our neighborhood. We pass laws, build walls, and turn away from our fellow human beings. We fail to see the image of God in the faces of newcomers, immigrants, and refugees.

The author of the Book of Hebrews wrote, "Don't forget to show friendship and welcome to strangers. Some people who have opened their homes and hearts to strangers have actually entertained angels." God's angels—Divine message-bearers—are everywhere, including within people who are unfamiliar to us. May we always be willing to welcome them, and may the prayers in this chapter remind us to reach out our hands to help in whatever ways we can.

Hospitality means primarily
the creation of free space
where the stranger can enter
and become a friend instead of an enemy.
Hospitality is not to change people,
but to offer them space where . . .
freedom [is] not disturbed by dividing lines.

—Henri J. M. Nouwen[10]

We raise our hands
and bless the hungry and the poor.
We lay these hands
to tend the hurting and the sore.
We stretch out these hands
to welcome the stranger at the door.

God who weeps over the city,
may we know the abandoned places,
may we sense the destructive patterns,
may we feel the suffering groups.
May we confess the ravages and rage.
May we embrace the hopes and despairs.

Life-Giver, help me to take the time
to sit in the shoes of the other person,
to start from where they are,
to listen to what they feel,
to refrain from the too-hasty judgement
or the too-ready answer,
to smile and be gentle,
to do whatever I can to help,
and never collude with the slipshod
but to prayerfully reach out
to help and welcome and include.

Pardoner and Restorer,
help us to listen
to the stories of those who are inflamed,
without judgement and with empathy.
Help us to stay calm
and learn what we can,
without defensiveness or excuses.
Help us to be clear about what we can achieve,
not promise what we cannot deliver,
and take responsibility for what we can deliver.
If it is possible, help us to walk a mile
in the other's shoes,
and to want the best for them,
just as we do for ourselves.
Show us where we can reach our hands to help,
and where we can extend our arms in welcome.
Make us useful
to all who are marginalized, isolated,
misunderstood, and oppressed.

Christ, help us to see
each member of Your Body
as You see them.
May we support each person in their calling.
May we honour the weak.
May we relate well
to other members of the Body
as we make our own contributions.
May we learn to receive and give,
recognizing that we are all needed,
welcomed, and included
in Your Body.

Cherisher,
we place into Your hands
the children of the streets
and our broken families.
Show us practical ways to reach out and help
all who are estranged and homeless.
Grant us grace to see that which is of You
in a difficult family member,
even though it is hidden beneath ugly traits.
Help us to learn from failure,
be transparent about our fears,
work on our weaknesses,
and build good communication,
both with those who think like we do
and with those who don't.
Remind us not to expect a single person—
whether friend, partner, or child—
to supply us with everything we need
emotionally, socially, or spiritually.

May we give each other space
to dance and fly,
to withdraw and hibernate,
and to come together again refreshed.

Give us eyes to notice the needy
and the stranger at the door.
Give us hearts to embrace the unwanted,
the homeless, and the poor.
Give us minds to weave understanding
and truth to spread and store.
Give us hands to help in little things
and to serve forevermore.

May both our hearts and homes
be places of royal hospitality
where welcome and mercy abound.
May our hearts and hands
do the hard work required
to unlock the song in every mind
and nourish every hungry soul.

O God, You endowed Hilda
with gifts of prudence and strength
to govern as a wise mother
over a large and fractious family;
grant us now those same gifts
of prudence, strength, and wisdom,
that we may build bridges of understanding
between those with clashing views,
and that we may create shelters
of understanding and acceptance.
May our common life together
be sustained by the connecting power
of Your Spirit.

Prayers of Self-Surrender

We often don't like to think in terms of self-surrender. After all, isn't "to surrender" the opposite of "to win"? Doesn't it mean we've given up?

But that kind of thinking, arising out of our cultural assumptions, is contrary to Christ's teaching in the Gospels. Ego says, "Me first." It insists, "I want the biggest piece. I deserve to have the best and most." This is the kind of thinking that lies at the very foundation of every act of injustice in our world, and it is the attitude that has created systems of privilege for some while others suffer inequity and injustice. Meanwhile, the Gospels teach that justice is built on the ego's surrender. When we love others as ourself (Matthew 22:26–39), treating them as we would want to be treated, we shift our priorities. We no longer see ourselves as the center of the world.

"Spiritual surrender is not passive resignation," wrote Deepak Chopra. "It is not giving up on life, it is letting go of the ego's agenda to get its way and allowing the impulse of action, creativity and inspiration from your soul to come through more strongly. Spiritual surrender actually requires more strength, love, courage, and honesty than what the ego sees as its push for justice, respect and recognition."[11]

Mary Beth Moze believes self-surrender is essential for transformation (both interior and exterior). We cannot begin to change either ourselves or our world until we are willing to give up our desire to be in control, to acquire, to accumulate. Dr. Moze points out that in Western culture, we perceive our heroes as all-powerful conquerors, while in indigenous societies, including the ancient Celtic culture, the hero is often wounded; she appears weak, for she has surrendered everything she once claimed would make her strong, and she ventures into the unknown in order to acquire wisdom she can bring back to humbly help and heal the community.[12]

May the prayers in this chapter give us the courage to surrender our selfish egos, as we too venture into the unknown, seeking the insights we need to heal our world.

*The secret of liberation in action
lies in doing all works without the ego-sense.
Here what is demanded of us is perfect self-surrender
through dedication of all our actions
to the Master power that controls the universe.*

—Samarth Ramdas[13]

Incomparable Guide,
Help us to travel light
and so be free from ego
and know the joy of discovery.
Help us to shed prejudice,
and so be strangers no longer
but pilgrims together.
Help us to stop trying to control,
and so let things happen
and to find You in the journeying.

May the Christ who walks
with wounded feet
walk with us on the road;
may we surrender our insistence on the easy route.
May the Christ who serves
with wounded hands
stretch out our hands to serve;
may we be willing to adjust ourselves
to the needs of others.
May the Christ who loves
with the wounded heart
open our hearts to love;
may we love without condition.

Jesus, You were driven to the desert
by the searching Spirit;
may we too be willing to go into the places
where we can be stripped
from what is not of You.
Forgive us
for our selfish deeds,
our empty speech,
and the words with which
we have wounded others.
Forgive us
for our false desires
and vengeful attitudes.
Free us
from our egos,
so that we can attend
to the needs of others.

Giver of all life and joy,
break open the shell of our selfishness.
Increase our desire
to enter into the world's life.
Make us secure enough to be with others.
Lead us into the deep connection
of the Divine-human cord
so that we are free to love
as You do.

In our pleasures,
Your kingdom come.
In our work,
Your kingdom come.
In our gatherings,
Your kingdom come.
On the roads,
Your kingdom come.
In each thing we do this day,
Your kingdom come.
Let us surrender our own selfish desires,
so Your kingdom come.

Set us free, O God,
from the selfish ego
that holds us back
from doing Your work.
Set us free
to put ourselves in others' shoes,
to be open to others' stories,
and to be sensitive to others in our speech,
See us free, O God,
from self-centeredness
that we may see Christ
in the face of each person we meet.
Set us free, O God,
from our fears and anxiety,
so that we may be willing
to cross barriers for You
as You crossed barriers for us.

Holy Trinity,
as You yield to one another,
may we yield to You
in each person we meet.
Help us to acquire
a deep, God-given awareness of others
that overwhelms our self-preoccupation,
so that we may build
the foundations of unity
and friendship.

Lead, me, Life-Giver,
into a place of prayer
where I live simply, silently,
and alone with You,
so that I may die to my selfishness
and Christ may grow in me;
so that You may give more of Yourself
through me
to a world that hungers for You.

(Inspired by words of Catherine Doherty.)

When I say, "Don't!"
would You say it like that, Jesus?
When I say, "Them,"
would You say it like that, Jesus?
When I say "I," would You,
who called Yourself "I Am,"
strain and push like that?
Break my brittle shell, Jesus,
and make me as human as You.

God of love,
I ask that You open my eyes each day,
so that I might see past my own needs,
and see others who are in need:
a child in the street, bullied or excluded;
someone at work, suffering or mistreated;
the older person on the bus, lonely and forgotten;
the person in the neighborhood,
rejected for their skin color or gender choices.
Teach me to be generous,
to give and not to count the cost.

Prayers for Energy and Empowerment

The fight for justice is neither fast nor easy. It has been going on since before we were born, and future generations will carry on the struggle when we are dead. We will win battles along the way, but the war itself continues, for oppression and injustice are like a thousand-headed hydra: as fast as we cut off one head, another grows. We must remain vigilant, constantly committed to the ongoing cause of bringing Divine justice to our world.

Understandably, however, at times we will become exhausted and discouraged. After all we are only human! Our strength is limited.

But God's strength has no limits. We can rely on the Creator to energize us when we are tired and empower us when we are weak. When we are burned out, tempted to give up, the Giver of Life yearns to renew us with a Mother's gentle love and a Father's encouraging strength. May these prayers by Ray Simpson remind us to seek Divine help when our own resources are gone.

Don't you know?
Haven't you heard?
The ancient and ever-new God,
the Life-Giver,
the one who shaped every corner of the world,
never grows weary or weak....
The Creator gives power
to those who have used up all their energy,
the Creator gives vigor and substance
to those who lack interior resources.
Even the young athletes may stumble from exhaustion,
but everyone who turns to the Life-Giver for help
will receive new energy.
They will fly on wings like eagles,
they will run without getting out of breath,
and they will be active without running out of steam.

—Isaiah 40:28–31

Break the ties that bind us to our past;
free us to go wherever You direct.
Bless the tiredness
that blinds us to Your presence;
grace us with
the scents of the company of heaven.
Burden us with the evils
that would ravage Your children;
spur us to struggle until the tide is turned.

God of the endless forcefield,
sow confusion in those
who would use terror
as a means of change.
Stir conviction in those
who can bring change
by acting justly
and by the sharing of love.

May our feet follow our hearts
until we find our place of resurrection:
the place where we are in harmony with ourselves,
our neighbours, our environment, and our God;
the context in which our creativity flows;
and the environment where our investment of love
will bear eternal fruit.

Life-Giver,
give us the statesmanship of the humble heart
and the willingness to move out toward others.
Give us the faith to do our bit
so that we may help to build a civilization of love.
Remind us that even the smallest acts
can help to bring about needed change.
Encourage us and empower us with Your Spirit.

Energize us with Your compassion,
Giver of Life,
to help the dispossessed,
to listen to those without voices,
and to reach out in friendship to all.
Teach those of us who live in comfort
to disarm terrorists through repentance
rather than force;
empower us with Your love;
encourage us with Your Spirit;
make us strong to bring Your justice
to individuals, communities, nations,
and the entire globe.

Holy Spirit, renew in us
joy in our work,
life in our being,
love in our relationships.
Noble Christ, take from us
cynicism, the need for control,
and mindless chatter.
Give to us wholeheartedness,
awareness, and compassion.
May we be a sacrament of strength
to those whose hands we hold,
as Your strong-fingered hands hold us.
Strengthen our resolve,
sharpen our minds, shape our wills,
grace our land with the justice
that's built from commitment
and the willingness to change.

Great Heart,
who reaches out to all,
energize our every nerve and sinew
to reach out to others with Your love.
May we accept each person as Yours.
May we include each person in our hearts.
May we find the strength to walk
with those who stumble,
to watch with those who suffer,
and to work with those who avoid us.

We need Your help, Spirit.
Inspire us, empower us, enlighten us.
Give us wise leaders, clear vision,
and an understanding of what is right.
Inspire in us true values.
Empower us to know ourselves,
know what is good
and know when to stop
and when to start.
As we work toward a world
that's free of prejudice, hate, and fear,
enlighten us with compassion and tolerance.
May we open our hearts to joy,
so that a thousand new flowers bloom,
and teach us to delight
in one another's creativity.
May our foreign policy be
to earn the trust and gratitude
of our neighbours.

Remind us to honour one another,
seek the common good,
and live as fellow citizens
of Your eternal kingdom.
Make us wise in our understanding,
open in our listening,
generous in our giving,
and vulnerable in our sharing.
Inspire us, empower us, and enlighten us
with Your Spirit.

May the love of the Three
empower a new community.
May the yielding of the Three
energize a new humanity.
May the life of the Three
inspire a new creativity.
May the togetherness of the Three
show us the way to a new unity.
May the glory of the Three
establish a new society.

Prayers of Blessing

God seeks to bless our world with good things—with peace and health, abundance and well-being—and we are called to participate in this ongoing work of Divine blessing. This means we strive always to bring about ever-greater goodness and wholeness in the lives of others. Instead of reacting in anger or hatred, we respond out of a genuine, deep-seated desire that each person in the world has opportunities to reach their full potential. We seek to create a society where everyone has what they need to thrive, and we work to bring about healing and justice in the lives of everyone we encounter. "Bless those who persecute and oppress, bless them and work for their well-being, and do not curse them or wish them harm," wrote the Apostle Paul (Romans 12:14).

May we use the prayers in this chapter to guide our thoughts and attitudes, so that we seek always to bless, bringing justice and freedom to each person in our world.

We are here to bless and prosper each other.

—Louise Hay[14]

*With each blessing uttered,
we extend the boundaries of the sacred
and ritualize our love of life.
One hundred times a day.
Everywhere we turn,
everything we touch, everyone we see.
The blessing can be whispered.
No one even needs to hear.
No one but the Holy One.
"Holy One of Blessing,
your Presence fills the universe.
Your Presence fills me."*

—Lawrence Kushner[15]

Bring to flower in Your children
the seeds that dormant lie.
In those who have none to encourage them,
bring the seeds of confidence to flower.
In those who are trapped by their circumstances,
bring the seeds of possibility to flower.
In those who find it difficult to learn,
bring the seeds of understanding to flower.
In those at the bottom of the social pile,
bring the seeds of empowerment to flower.

We pray to You for the places of desecration:
bring forth beauty from them.
We pray to You for the hard and barren places:
bring forth generosity from them.
We pray to You for the greed- and guilt-laden places:
bring forth healing in them,
and let Your love and life bloom there.

We pray for:
the financial moguls
who give a bit to charity
but milk the most vulnerable dry;
the media moguls
who run down struggling public servants
and destroy rivals without a blink;
celebrities who smile nicely on camera
and abuse others when out of sight.
Give us clarity about what is right
and courage to confront what is wrong.
May we do this in such a way
that these individuals know
we truly care for them
and not only for those they abuse.

May our sons grow up strong and
straight like young trees.
May our daughters have the beauty of inner strength.
May our farms and industries overflow.
May the voice of complaining cease from our streets.
Happy are the people from whom such blessings flow
who put their trust in God.

(Inspired by Psalm 144.)

We pray for this land
and for her children, whatever their faith:
Buddhists and Muslims,
Pagans and Christians,
Hindus and all other religions,
believers and atheists.
We pray for our nation's prisoners,
including prisoners of prejudice, pride, and poverty,
as well as prisoners of addiction and self-doubt.
We pray for our country's hospitals,
for those who are injured and ailing
and for those who treat them and care for them.
We pray for our land's extraverts and introverts
for her famous people
and her forgotten or overlooked people.
And we pray our nation may journey
from fragmentation and inequity
toward wholeness and equality.

Caring Provider,
in You we each live and move
and have our being;
You have given us all we need
through the interwoven web of life.
Sustain those
who delve for the Earth's minerals,
grow crops, or rear cattle.
Bless those who create textiles,
drive trucks and trains and buses,
or clean our streets and businesses.
Give wisdom
to those who create and manage technology
that they may do so for the world's good.
Bless all work done today
that enables the human family
to be clothed, fed, and housed in dignity.
receive a fair return for work,
and celebrate the gift of life.

God of community,
we pray for the powerful
who impose their will on the weak;
may they come to know Your defenseless love.
We pray for those who seek revenge
through acts of terror;
may they come to know Your unconditional love.
We pray for those who have lost jobs or homes,
liberty or loved ones;
may they come to know Your abundant love.
We pray for those who are oppressed and suffering;
may they come to know Your empowering love.
Bring to birth, we pray, a community
that's built on justice.

God, we pray Your blessing
on the consequences of our actions:
save others' from our vileness,
and save them from our "niceness."
Save them from our hardness,
and from our deafness.
And save us too, we pray:
from our vileness and from our "niceness,"
our hardness and our deafness.
God save the people:
save us from our nemesis,
save us from ourselves.

We pray for those who are unable
to find the paid work they desire;
may they know You will accompany them
as they give their best from day to day.
We pray for employers and community builders;
may they generate energy, ideas,
and new possibilities of employment.
We pray for those
whose opportunities have been curtailed,
by prejudice or poverty;
may we look for ways to bless them
with our words and hands
and hearts.

Guardian,
be over the restless people
a covering of truth and peace.
Bless where there is fear,
bless where there is hatred,
bless where there is anything
that separates us from each other.
Lover of all souls,
watch over us
and keep us true in all we do.

Bless, Life-Giver,
our government and civic leaders.
May they be shepherds of their people,
not self-serving;
alert to needs, not apathetic;
strategic for the long-term good work,
not blown off course by every wind;
friends of the whole human family,
and not prejudiced or partisan.

Christ who holds all things together,
before You died
You prayed for the unity of all who believe.
We join You in Your prayer
so that all peoples
attain communion
around one table on Earth.
Bless our local communities
and inspire neighbours to love others
as themselves.
Bless us, we pray,
and make us signs of Your presence
that transforms all Creation.

God bless the stranger at the door.
God bless the baby on the floor.
God bless the shopper, piled with goods.
God bless teenagers masked in hoods.
God bless the preoccupied business gent.
God bless the old woman, lined and bent.
God bless us all—one family,
love-encompassed in Trinity.

God bless Muslims
and God bless Christians.
God bless Hindus
and God bless Jews.
God bless atheists
and God bless Pagans.
God bless young people
and God bless old people.
God bless people with different abilities
and God bless every size and shape of body.
God bless Black people
and God bless white people.
God bless brown people
and God bless ALL people.
Bless our enemies and bless our neighbours.
Bless our leaders and those who have no voice.
Change their hearts.
Change our hearts.
And let all the people say:
Amen.

Bless our world, Life-Giver,
for the nations rage
and people around us become vengeful.
May the realms of this world
be united in Your kingdom.
Bless us as we confront
a world of selfishness and separation.
Help us work for justice
with the calm assurance and quiet confidence
of the Risen Christ.
Bless as we do what we can,
and leave the rest to You.

We pray for all people:
their patterns and their pastimes,
their work and their homes,
their lovemaking and their conflicts,
their dreams and their disillusionments,
their hopes and their eternal hungers.
Bless them all, we pray,
and use us to bless
and bring Your justice to all.

Christ of the scars of love,
into Your hands we place
those who have been scarred by life:
those who have been betrayed,
and those who have suffered loss of profession,
reputation, or self-esteem.
Christ of the scars of love,
into Your hands we place unwanted children,
neighbours defamed, lovers spurned,
and anyone who has been rejected
because of skin color, belief, or gender.
Christ of the scars of love,
into Your hands we place
those who are victims of violence,
unkind practice, or false accusation.
Bless and heal each wounded person,
for we know
by Your scars,
we are all healed.

Healing power of Christ,
penetrate the brittle shells
of the ones for whom we pray.
Where others no longer seem to see them,
attract them to Your gaze.
Where they are down and out,
grasp hold of them and raise them up.
Where they are fettered,
set them free to leap and praise.

On those who harbour fear,
    come, Holy Spirit.
On those whose day is drab,
    come, Holy Spirit.
On those whose lives are parched,
    come, Holy Spirit.
On those who suffer injustice and oppression,
    come, Holy Spirit.

Life-Giver, Pain-Bearer,
we offer You our tears
for those broken by abuse
and our anguish for those who die in our streets,
victims of prejudice, cruelty, and hatred.
We offer You the burdens we carry
for the needy and poor.
May our sufferings contribute to the suffering
that Your universal body needs to complete
in order to transform
every last person and place on Earth.
May our pain be useful to Your plan
to redeem our world,
and may our sorrow be contained by Your love
so that we bless others
with both our hearts
and our hands.

Mother-God of loving care,
bless these battered children.
Take the pain out of their bodies.
Take the fear out of their lives.
Take the despair out of their hearts.
Take the resentment out of their minds.
Heal them and bless them
with Your gentle, healing love.
Gentle Father-God,
bless these battered children,
and may Your gentle Spirit flow
through all those who care for them.

Tender Saviour, Lover of our souls,
bless these battered women.
Take the pain out of their bodies.
Take the fear out of their lives.
Take the despair out of their hearts.
Take the resentment out of their minds.

Heal them and bless them
with Your gentle, healing love,
and may Your tender Spirit flow
through all those who know or care for them.

Caressing Spirit, Companion of our souls,
bless these elder ones
who feel battered by loneliness, rejection,
and the thoughtless cruelty of younger folk.
Take the pain out of their bodies.
Take the fear out of their lives.
Take the despair out of their hearts.
Take the resentment out of their minds.
Heal them and bless them
with Your gentle, healing love,
and may Your caressing Spirit flow
through all those who know or care for them.

God who is One,
You create us in diversity.
God who is Three,
You draw us into unity.
We give You thanks
for the little trinities
that reflect Your nature to us
in community.

We ask Your blessing on places
where community has been destroyed.
May the love of the Three
give birth to new community.
May the life of the Three
give birth to new creativity.
May the oneness of the Three
give birth to a new unity.

Endnotes

1. Margaret Klenck. "The Psychological and Spiritual Efficacy of Confession," *Journal of Religion and Health.* 43 (2: 2004), p. 139.

2. Quoted in Jenna Grey-Eagle, "Sustainability from an Indigenous Perspective," *Lower Phalen Creek Project* (May 9, 2022), https://www.lowerphalencreek.org/.

3. Ibid.

4. Nicholas Stern. *Stern Review on the Economics of Climate Change* (London: Government of the United Kingdom, 2006), p. iv.

5. Matthew Fox. "Ninety-Five Theses," *A New Reformation: Creation Spirituality and the Transformation of Christianity* (Rochester, VT: Inner Traditions, 2006), #19.

6. Thomas Berry. *The Great Work: Our Way into the Future* (New York: Harmony/Bell Tower, 1999), p. 82.

7. Desmond Tutu. *No Future Without Forgiveness* (New York: Image), p. 39.

8. Martin Luther King Jr. Speech given at the National Conference of Religion and Race (Chicago, 1963).

9. Oscar Romero. *The Violence of Love* (Maryknoll, NY: Orbis, 2004), December 31, 1977 entry.

10. Henri J. M. Nouwen. *Reaching Out: The Three Movements of the Spiritual Life* (New York: Image, 1986), p. 51.

11. Deepak Chopra. "Surrender or Keep Pushing," *Ask Deepak* (December 17, 2020), https://www.deepakchopra.com/.

12. Mary Beth G. Moze. "Surrender: An Alchemical Act in Personal Transformation" *Journal of Conscious Evolution 3* (3: 2007), p. 7.

13. Samarth Ramdas. *In the Vision of God* (San Francisco, CA: Sufi Ruhaniat International, 2017), p. 438. (Ramdas was a seventeenth-century Hindu saint.)

14. Louise Hay. *Trust Life: Love Yourself Everyday with Wisdom from Wisdom from Louise Hay* (Carlsbad, CA: Hay House, 2017), p. 17.

15. Lawrence Kushner. *The Book of Words: Talking Spiritual Life, Living Spiritual Talk* (Woodstock, VT: LongHill, 1993), p. 20.

More books on
Celtic spirituality
that are also by
RAY SIMPSON...

(All are available from Anamchara Books.
Amazon, and most online booksellers.)

Dance of Creation
Celtic Prayers of Celebration and Insight, Repentance and Restoration

In the prayers collected in this book, Ray Simpson asks us to "hear the cry of the earth and work together to choose life" (Deuteronomy 30:19). He reminds us that Divine life courses through Earth's rivers, breathes through her winds, and sings in each life form she nourishes, and he invites us to celebrate Earth's beauty as we learn from her deep wisdom. At the same time, with a prophet's clear voice, he calls to us to repent of our selfishness and ignorance, and commit ourselves to the Earth's healing and restoration. "Come!" he says. "Celebrate! Learn! Repent! Take hands and work together! Join in Creation's dance with all your strength and soul!"

*May every soul join
with the song
Nature sings.
May the birds sing,
may the trees clap,
and may we humans
taste and dance.*

Tree of Life
Celtic Prayers to the Universal Christ

**Christ is the visible image of the invisible God.
He existed before anything was created and is supreme
over all creation, for through him God created
everything.... He existed before anything else,
and he holds all creation together.**
—*Colossians 1:15–17*

Like a vast, ever-growing Tree of Life, Christ—the expression of Divine love—expands endlessly throughout the universe. This is the perspective of ancient Celtic spirituality, and it is this concept that Ray Simpson reveals in his poem-prayers. Inspired by the traditional Celtic style of prayer, he gives words to our individual relationships with God. He speaks of the wonder, beauty, and love revealed through the Universal Christ, the Tree of Life that includes all that is. Each and everything in creation is sacred, for everything is a word of God—and we too are called to be God's words to our world.

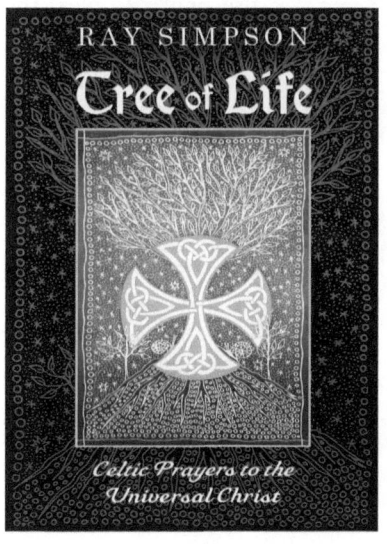

Celtic Prayers for the Rhythm of Each Day

**Every hour is holy,
every day is sacred**

We sometimes think prayer belongs only in certain places on certain days. This book calls us to set prayer free from these constraints, allowing it to flow out through the hours of every workday, sanctifying the ordinary rhythm of our modern lives.

Ray Simpson gives us twenty original prayers, written in the Celtic tradition or patterned after ancient Celtic prayers, for each interval of the day. Like generations of earlier followers of Christ, we too can use prayer to bless the rhythm of our daily lives, infusing the hours with the awareness of the One who gives us Life. These small pauses throughout the day will make us ever more aware that the Kingdom of Heaven is a constant and present reality, hidden just beneath the veil of everyday life.

The Celtic Book of Days

*Ancient Wisdom for Each Day
of the Year from the
Celtic Followers of Christ*

**This book will change
the way you look at everyday life.**

The ancient Celts found God's presence in each ordinary moment of the day. Everything they encountered revealed to them the presence of the sacred; each day was deep with meaning. Now you too can practice the Celts' faith, as you take a few moments to immerse yourself in their wisdom. These small daily moments of reflection and insight will open your heart to each day and all it holds.

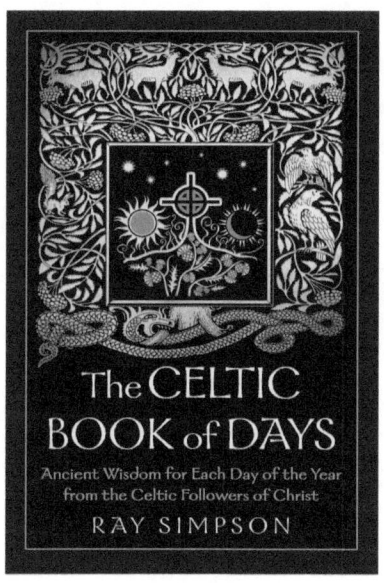

Celtic Christianity
Deep Roots for a Modern Faith

Celtic Spirituality for the Modern World

The world of the long-ago Celts appeals to many of us in the twenty-first century. Whether we are looking to find our cultural heritage or are seeking an alternative to worn and restrictive religious forms, the earth-centered, woman-friendly, inclusive faith of the Christian Celts offers us a deep-rooted alternative approach to traditional Christianity. The Celts experienced "thin places," where they sensed the supernatural world; they honored their poets, singers, and artists; and they passionately followed the Christ of the Gospels. Theirs was a church without walls, which lived naturally and comfortably within the community. Ray Simpson has spent most of his life walking in the footsteps of the Christian Celts, and now he allows us to experience for ourselves their dynamic spirituality.

Soul Friendship in the Celtic Tradition
Ancient Insights for Today

The special friend who accompanies a person through life's journey is more precious than gold. The early Christian Celts had a heartwarming name for this person: the Anamchara. (Anam is the Gaelic word for soul; chara is the word for friend—"friend of the soul.") This special friend was someone with whom a person could talk through practical matters, reveal hidden intimacies, and break through the barriers of convention and egotism to an eternal unity of soul.

Ray Simpson brings this ancient concept into the twenty-first century, drawing practical applications from the long history of soul friendship. He describes a spiritual bond that lasts beyond this life into eternity, for it flows directly from God, who is the pattern of all friendship, the center and source of all human relationships.